OCTOPUS

LIVING THINGS

OCTOPUS

Rebecca Stefoff

BENCHMARK BOOKS

MARSHALL CAVENDISH
NEW YORK

Benchmark Books
Marshall Cavendish Corporation
99 White Plains Road
Tarrytown, New York 10591-9001

Text copyright © 1997 by Rebecca Stefoff
Illustrations copyright © by Marshall Cavendish Corporation
All rights reserved. No part of this book may be reproduced in any form
without written permission from the publisher.

Illustrations by Jean Cassels

Library of Congress Cataloging-in-Publication Data
Stefoff, Rebecca   date
Octopus / by Rebecca Stefoff.
p.   cm. — (Living things)
Includes bibliographical references and index.
Summary: Describes the physical characteristics, behavior,
and habitat of octopuses and several similar creatures.
ISBN 0-7614-0119-9 (lib. bdg.)
1. Octopus—Juvenile literature. [1.Octopus.] I. Title
II. Series: Stefoff, Rebecca date   Living things.
QL430.302S88   1997   594'.56—dc20   96-1131 CIP AC

Photo research by Ellen Barrett Dudley

Cover photo: *Tom Stack and Associates*

The photographs in this book are used by permission and through the courtesy of
Tom Stack and Associates: 2, 10, 11 (bottom), 12 (bottom), 15 (top), 16, 24.
Peter Arnold: Fred Bavendam, 6-7, 19 (left and right), 20, 25 (right), 26 (left);
Kelvin Aitkin, 9 (bottom), 11 (top); Lynn Funkhouser, 11 (middle); Schafer and Hill,
21. *Animals Animals:* Max Gibbs/Oxford Scientific Films, 8, 25 (left); G.I.
Bernard/Oxford Scientific Films, 9 (top); Zig Leszczynski, 12 (top); Francis
Abbott/Oxford Scientific Films, 13; Rodger Jackman/Oxford Scientific Films, 14;
Mark Deeble and Victoria Stone/Oxford Scientific Films, 15 (bottom); E.R.
Degginger, 18; Bruce Watkins, 32. *Photo Researchers, Inc.:* Nancy Sefton, 17;
Tony Angermayer, 22; Douglas Faulkner, 23; Sophie de Wilde/Jacana, 27 (right).

Printed in the United States of America

3   5   6   4   2

To Sarah Elizabeth Muntzing

Pacific giant octopus

The ocean is restless. On the sea bottom, a swift current flows across the sand like a wind blowing across the land.

Sea grass bends in the current. An animal is bending with the current too. What is it?

It is an octopus.

The octopus doesn't have bones to give it a shape. The octopus's body is like a loose, floppy bag. It's hard to know what an octopus really looks like, because its shape depends upon what it is doing.

common octopus

The octopus has eight long legs. Or are they arms? They're called tentacles. Octopuses use their tentacles for crawling and for picking up things.

A short tube called a funnel sticks out of the octopus's body. When the octopus wants to move fast, it fills its body with water and squirts the water out through the funnel. This pushes the octopus through the water.

Can you see the funnel on the octopus at the top of this page? Find the octopus's eye and then look below it.

A hungry octopus stretches its tentacles out in all directions. It pokes them into holes and under rocks, looking for food.

Australian octopus

day octopus

An octopus's skin can do many things. It can change color as fast as you can blink your eyes.

Octopuses are shy, gentle animals. But if an octopus becomes angry, it turns red or some other bright color. If the octopus is frightened, it turns light or dark.

blue-ringed octopus

Sometimes octopuses flash bright spots or stripes. They may be saying "Stay away from me!"

An octopus can change its shape. It can puff out its skin to make itself look bigger or spread itself flat on the seafloor.

octopus on Caribbean reef

Caribbean octopus at night

The octopus uses these tricks to hide from the whales, seals, and fish that want to eat it.

11

blue-ringed octopus in camouflage coloring

octopus at entrance to its hole

octopus squirting ink

The octopus has other ways of hiding. It can change the color of its skin to match its background. If you swam past, you would see the rocks and plants on the sea bottom. But would you see the octopus hiding among them?

Octopuses also hide in holes in the rocks. The octopus peeps out to watch the world go by. At the first sign of danger, it will pull its eyes and tentacles back into its hiding place.

If an octopus is attacked, it squirts a cloud of blackish liquid into the water. This surprises its enemy. Now the octopus can swim away to safety.

octopus's tentacle

The octopus's strong tentacles are covered with many round disks called suckers. The suckers help the octopus keep a tight grip on whatever it is holding.

The octopus can see very well with its large eyes. It can even wink, just like a person can. Imagine swimming past an octopus and seeing it wink at you!

close-up of suckers on a tentacle

eye of Pacific giant octopus

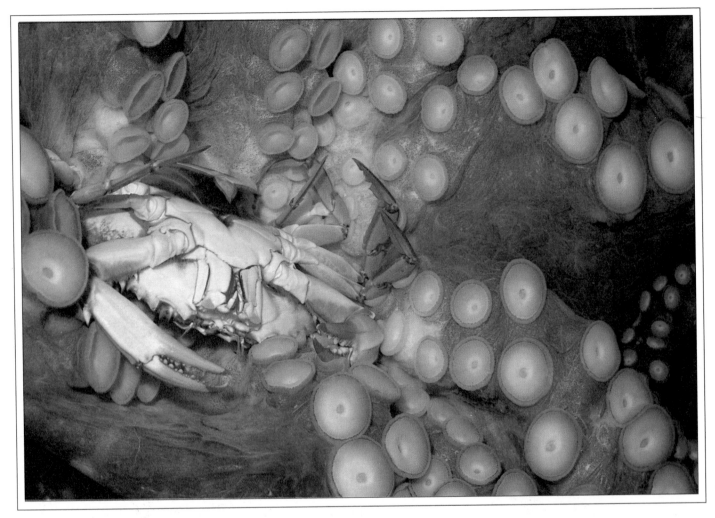

octopus eating a crab

When the octopus sees something that looks good to eat, it reaches out with its tentacles. The suckers hold the meal while the tentacles pull it toward the octopus's mouth.

The octopus's mouth is under its body. The mouth has a sharp beak like a bird's. The octopus uses this beak to crack the hard shells of crabs and clams, two of its favorite foods. Then, with its long, prickly tongue, the octopus scoops the meat out of the shells.

octopus preparing to eat a clam

Caribbean dwarf octopus

There are about one hundred different kinds of octopuses in the world's oceans. Some of them are tiny. The smallest octopuses are smaller than your hand when they are fully grown. The largest ones are bigger than a tall person.

Some octopuses live in shallow water. They swim near the top of the ocean. Other octopuses live far below, in the deep dark waters far from land.

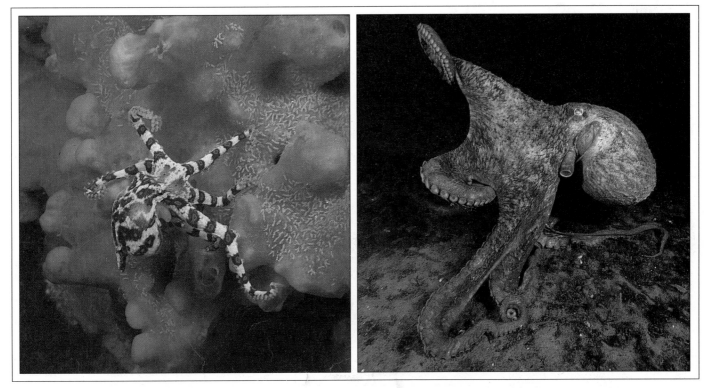

southern blue-ringed octopus   *Pacific giant octopus*

pinstripe squid

Octopuses aren't the only sea creatures with tentacles. Their cousins, the squid and the cuttlefish, also have them.

Squids and cuttlefish have ten tentacles each. But you might have a hard time counting them, because squids and cuttlefish like to swim with their tentacles pulled up close to their bodies.

giant cuttlefish

common cuttlefish

adult nautilus with young

The cuttlefish isn't loose and floppy like the octopus and the squid. Inside its body, the cuttlefish has a hard shell that looks and feels like chalk. This shell gives the cuttlefish's body its shape.

Another cousin of the octopus is called the nautilus. The nautilus has a shell, too, but its shell is outside its body. Do you see the ends of tentacles sticking out of the nautilus's beautiful curved shell? If you look closely, you can see the nautilus's eye peering out.

day octopuses mating

Octopuses live alone most of the time. But when it is time for them to have babies, two octopuses join together for a while.

24

octopus eggs   *female Pacific giant octopus guarding eggs*

The father octopus reaches under the mother octopus's skin with one of his tentacles.

Later the mother octopus lays thousands of eggs. The eggs look like grains of white rice hanging together in long ribbons.

For weeks, the mother octopus guards the eggs. She squirts clean water on them with her funnel and gently brushes away dirt with her suckers.

25

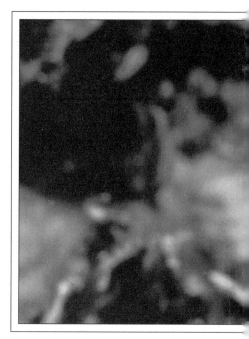

newborn octopus

Pacific giant octopus emerging from egg

At last the baby octopuses are ready to come into the world. The eggs burst open, and the tiny octopuses swim free.

The mother octopus will die soon after her eggs hatch. She will not see her babies again. They must face the dangers of the ocean on their own.

Many of the baby octopuses will be eaten by fish, sea birds, or other creatures. But a few lucky ones will live. They are small now, but they will grow. One day they will send their own baby octopuses swimming out into the world.

A QUICK LOOK AT THE OCTOPUS AND ITS RELATIVES

Octopuses, squids, cuttlefish, and nautiluses are invertebrates. This means that they are animals without skeletons, although they may have shells. Octopuses and their relatives belong to a special group of invertebrates called cephalopods (SEFF uh lo pods), which means "head-footed creatures." Scientists gave the cephalopods this name because they look like large heads with legs attached. Cephalopods—especially octopuses—are the most intelligent creatures in the sea, other than mammals.

Here are five kinds of cephalopods, with their scientific names and some key facts.

COMMON OCTOPUS

Octopus vulgaris
(OCK tuh puss vull GAHR iss)
Lives in holes and cracks in rocky sea bottoms in the Mediterranean Sea and the world's oceans, except in very cold water.

BLUE-RINGED OCTOPUS

Hapalochlaena maculosa
(hap uh lo CLY nah mack you LO sah)
Colorful octopus that lives in the waters near Australia. Like all octopuses, it is shy, but it will bite if threatened. Its bite is poisonous and has been known to kill humans.

PACIFIC GIANT OCTOPUS

Octopus dofleini

(OCK tuh puss doh FLAY nee)

World's largest octopus. Usually measures about 8 feet across (2.5 m) from tentacle tip to tentacle tip. Largest one ever found was more than 31 feet across (9.5 m). Lives off the coasts of British Columbia and Alaska.

GIANT CUTTLEFISH

Sepia apama

(SEE pee ah ah PAHM ah)

The largest cuttlefish. Grows up to 4 feet in length (1 m). Like all cuttlefish, has 10 tentacles and a chalklike shell inside its body. Lives in the waters off southern Australia.

ATLANTIC GIANT SQUID

Architeuthis princeps

(ark ih TYOO thiss PRIN sepps)

The world's largest cephalopod and largest invertebrate. Has been known to measure 60 feet (18 m) from top of head to tip of tentacles. Lives in the North Atlantic Ocean. Like all squid, has 10 tentacles.

Taking Care of the Octopus

Like all ocean-dwelling creatures, octopuses and their relatives need clean water to live in. Pollution of the oceans could make the seas unsafe for octopuses. These animals face another danger, too. People catch so many octopuses and squids to eat and to use as fishing bait that some kinds may disappear completely. These gentle, intelligent creatures need our protection.

Find Out More

Carrick, Carol. *Octopus*. New York: Seabury Press, 1978.

Lauber, Patricia. *An Octopus Is Amazing*. New York: Crowell, 1990.

Martin, James. *Tentacles: The Amazing World of Octopus, Squid, and Their Relatives*. New York: Crown, 1993.

Stephens, William M. *Octopus Lives in the Ocean*. New York: Holiday House, 1968.

Index

Rebecca Stefoff has published many books for young readers. Science and environmental issues are among her favorite subjects. She lives in Oregon and enjoys observing the natural world while hiking, camping, and scuba diving.

red octopus